THIS BOOK BELONGS TO :

_____

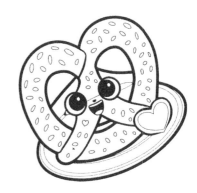

WELCOME TO A COZY CHRISTMAS ADVENTURE!

The holiday season is here, and so is the perfect time to relax, unwind, and indulge in some delightful coloring! "Cute Food in a Cozy Mood Christmas Coloring Book" is your cozy companion, designed to fill your days with joy and creativity.

Inside, you'll find adorable food characters getting into all sorts of festive fun —from singing carols to wrapping presents and warming up with hot cocoa. Every page is crafted to capture the magic of Christmas, bringing you a sense of comfort, laughter, and nostalgia. Whether it's a quiet winter evening or a cozy afternoon by the fire, this book is here to make your holidays even more special.

With simple, bold outlines and cheerful designs, this coloring book is perfect for adding your own splash of color to the Christmas spirit. There's no need to rush—take your time, find your favorite colors, and let each illustration come to life in your own unique way.

So, grab your coloring tools, settle into your favorite cozy spot, and let the festive journey begin!

HAPPY HOLIDAYS AND MERRY COLORING!

40 WONDERFUL SCENES YOU'LL FIND INSIDE :

A Jolly Coloring Tip!

Ho, ho, ho! 🎅

Before you start bringing these pages to life with your favorite colors, here's a little tip to keep each masterpiece merry and bright! 🌟

Slip a blank sheet of paper or even better, a piece of cardboard under the page you're working on. This extra layer is like a holiday guardian, protecting your other pages from any color bleed-through—especially if you're using markers! 🎨

So go ahead, color away with all the festive joy, knowing that every page will shine as the work of art it was meant to be! 🎄✨

Santa's Color Test! 🎨

Try your colors here with Santa! ✏️ Find the perfect shades before you color your holiday masterpiece! 🎅

THANK YOU! 🎄

We hope this coloring book brought you as much joy and relaxation as we felt creating it for you! 🥰   We aimed to exceed your expectations, and we hope each page left you with a smile and a heart full of holiday cheer. 🫶⭐

If you enjoyed this coloring journey, we would be so grateful if you could leave a review! 📖✨   Your feedback helps our book reach more colorists, spreading joy and creativity throughout the holiday season. 🎨

Wishing you a bright, colorful, and wonderful holiday season!!! 🎁 🎄

With gratitude,

Andrea Sylvia

Made in the USA
Monee, IL
25 November 2024